Jus Mee

By Jus Mee

Jus Mee

Composed by Jus Mee

Cover Created by Jazzy Kitty Publications

Logo Designs by Andre M. Saunders/Leroy Grayson

Editor: Anelda Attaway

© 2021 Jus Mee

ISBN 978-1-954425-15-6

Library of Congress Control Number: 2021903248

All rights reserved. This book is protected by the copyright laws of the United States of America. This book may not be copied or reprinted for commercial gain or profit. The use of short quotations or occasional page copying for personal or group study is permitted and encouraged. Permission will be granted upon request. For Worldwide Distribution. Printed in the United States of America. Published by Jazzy Kitty Publications utilizing Microsoft Publishing Software and Bookcover Pro. The Holy Scriptures are from the Holy Bible.

DEDICATION

This is dedicated to Eulee and Lou Lou.

TABLE OF CONTENTS

Introduction i
Down but Not Broken 01
    Depression 1 02
    I Need to Marry a Poet 05
    Clarity 11
Erotic 15
    I Gave You Passion 16
The First 19
    It All Came Out 20
    Water 25
    Sometimes I Just Write 28
Work Chronicles 31
    The Cubicles 32
A Birthday Party for Jesus 37
    Because He Rose 38
    The Nativity of Jesus 40
Conclusion 42
    My Day 44
    Be Happy 46
About the Author 49

INTRODUCTION
Welcome!

This book is a small compilation, showing various sides of Mee.

It is my first published book, showing different times in my life and different obstacles that I overcame. I am expressing myself through the art form of poetry. My mother always says that I "dance to the beat of my own drum." I pride myself on being my own person and being different from the rest. I work every day on getting to know and love Mee better.

I am reminded of a saying that I was taught by my mother from a very young age. The more I say it, the more I believe it to be true:

"Never follow the crowd, look where the millions stop. You will always find the crowd at the base. There is always room at the top." Author unknown.

DOWN BUT NOT BROKEN

For a few years, I suffered from depression. I didn't realize what was going on in my life until I sat myself down and decided that I didn't want to feel the way I felt any longer. Although it is a constant battle to try and not let depression get the best of me, I feel better now.

The first poem is called Depression 1. I wrote this poem on October 14, 2013. The second poem was written on February 8, 2011 at 7am.

There are a few more poems in this chapter, but the dates are not available. I do know that 2011 - 2014 were tough years for me. The poems may come across as a bit dark, because at the time, I was dealing with a stressful relationship. I put loving him, before loving me.

DEPRESSION 1

It's funny how things change within the blink of an eye.

Or how u hear that song that makes you cry.

How u react to that dude that passes by

And u turn to your girl and say, "Yo he's fly!"

Or how the people u love most can make u cry.

Or how the ones u are the closest to, just up and die.

And you're left alone, just wondering why?

And they got the nerve to judge' when you're just living your life.

Or how the packs u got, just ain't cut right.

And your dreams of a come up, just vanished overnight.

So, u go to church on a Sunday cuz u know u ain't living right.

But secretly ur just wishing it was Saturday night.

Cuz all u really want to do is pop bottles and front all night.

Then Wednesday comes, no funds for the lights.

You bout to have a kid by a dude who potentially has a wife.

Your dad ain't around, mom frowns cuz u living that trife life.

When u know your purpose is to be a mom and a wife.

U catching public transportation cuz the dude u sleepin' wit got your ride.

And u gave it to him cuz u got hopes of being his bride.

Then u sitting in your room and you're all alone.

Can't nobody call u, u ain't pay the bill so u ain't got no phone.

But u waiting for it to ring, even though there's no dial tone.

U open the fridge and there's no food.

U look for ur dude but he's riding around with his boys in your whip in some hood.

So, u think about how u got to this point.

Don't have money for blunts so u spark up a joint.

Can't get high, cuz it ain't that loud

It's like u a rapper performing for no crowd.

You feel worthless, helpless, a lost soul with misguided direction.

Sleeping with this dude with no protection

It's like sucking a dick that can't get an erection.

But it's never too late to change up lanes

We all go through life with growing pains

And one thing for sure

It will always remain the same

Like Marlo said from the wire

"My name is my name"

And the moral of this is

You are a reflection of u

U holding a grudge because of what u decided to do

And at the end of the day

U can only be mad at u.

Ain't nobody go straight to the top

We all gotta go through

So stop feeling sorry for yourself

And do what u gotta do.

So don't judge me and I won't judge u

I NEED TO MARRY A POET

Well,

just maybe I need to get me a man who understands poetry,

yeah,

I want a poet,

that way, he will look at me and see that I am not as complicated as the words that he uses in his poems.

I am a storybook,

a page turner,

a hot commodity who owns a property with no kids.

Not trying to be the best on the mic or get noticed for my poetry,

just doing what I love and sharing what keeps me up at night with everyone I know.

Maybe he will recognize around page 23,

that I devoted years of my life to a relationship that would never be

and somehow got into the habit of letting people who are so insignificant in my life judge me,

and I let their words hurt me,

repeatedly,

this all started at page 23.

Or maybe he will turn to page 7

and realize that this was the age that I could first recall experiencing death

although it didn't seem to affect me until page 9 when I lost my uncle and my papa and I saw my daddy cry.

Or maybe he will turn to page 16 when I thought I was really in love.

And on page 16 I put my boyfriend, before everything,

even my schoolwork.

And where I was once an A student, I argued with my mother and tried to convince her that she needed to accept me anyway, because maybe I was just a C student now (I learned that from Theo on the Cosby's)

Or maybe, he will read pages 17, 25, and 28 and realize that I still miss my babies everyday

even though God saw it best that they come home to him and in my mind,

I have already convinced myself that they were ANGELS, and that this good old EARTH, really wasn't deserving of them anyway, that's just how I cope.

Or maybe,

just maybe he will turn to page 30 and realize that he will never understand how it feels to have your favorite panties torn from off of your body and be given scars that would take nearly 5 years to leave your skin.

Or how it feels to be forced into really doing something that you don't want to do, but you give in,

as you watch the clock,

or like someone with OCD, you count numbers in your head to take your mind off of this body, taking your body and doing what they want to do with it,

even though you said no.

Maybe by the end of page 30 he will realize why forgiveness is a learning process for me

and when he turns to page 31, he will understand why I am working on not holding a grudge,

and by the middle of 31, he will realize that to me,

LOVE is more important than SEX.

And that if he just gives me a little more time, I will love him unconditionally but I just have to trust, that his touch will not be offensive.

In any event, he will understand me, because my life is like a story book.

He will know by page 32, that it took me 32 years of my life,

to realize that the most important man in my life is my father,

even though when I lived in the same house with him, he didn't even speak to me most days but I didn't realize how much I loved him until I almost lost him, and I am glad that I didn't lose him because even though he may not remember, 2 seconds after I say it, I still have another chance to tell my Daddy everything that I want to say, and I know a lot of people who can't do the same.

My Dad is the strongest man that I know, because he is still living after 5 heart attacks in 1 night,

he is special, and he's my family's miracle

and this poet, MUST possess some of my father's qualities, or our conversation will end at "shorty, where's your man at."

And in my mind, I will hear my Mother's words "Behind that preposition "AT." and my poet, my man, my true love, will understand that.

And instead of 2 snaps, he will look at me like I am a story book,

one of his favorite books, and he will place me high up on a shelf,

to signal to the others that only he can hold this book in his hands,

it means something to him,

he won't be lending this book out,

and he will always want to read it

and he will think

"she is not that complicated,

she is deep,

but it's all normal,

and I want to comfort her,

tell her it will be Ok,

because I love her,

and the moment I decided to read this book, I felt a connection, because she didn't hesitate to dedicate this book to me,

before I even read her.

She knew I was coming

she knew in her heart, that she would deem me worthy,

and that this would be a book, that I wouldn't want to share with anyone else,

because only I would know how to receive these words on these pages,

because I am a poet,

and I use big words,

but with her,

everything is simple.

and reading her, is my favorite pass time."

CLARITY

I was afraid to let you touch me,

I hadn't been touched in so long.

I was afraid for you to love me,

I felt like in the past, I had been loved so wrong.

I was afraid to let down my guard and share all of me with you.

I was afraid that if I did, you might put me through some type of mental abuse.

I was afraid to talk things out, for fear of hearing that I nag too much.

And I was afraid to tell you what I was feeling, for fear that you would feel rushed.

I was afraid to meet your family, because I never felt like you wanted me too.

I was ashamed of my complexion, because you reminded me I was too light for you.

I often wondered why I gave in when I did.

I think that I was just lonely.

I figured that I could make things work, and maybe certain things would just grow on me.

The fact that I spent holidays, and many nights alone.

Or the times that I would call you and another woman would pick up your phone.

And then there was the time that you said you were going to visit your kids.

I went to the supermarket and decided to ride past your crib.

Although it was raining, I could see that your lights were on.

So, I figured maybe he didn't leave, maybe I should honk the horn.

And even though it was raining out, a woman came out with a bonnet on her head.

She stared into my car, looked up at your window and I just shook my head.

So, she was the one that's been sleeping in your bed?

Because I can't even remember the last time, I stayed with you.

And now that I think about it, you have been coming to my house to stay whenever you want to.

And let's not talk about the packs that I risked my life to bring back to our state.

You didn't even break me off, you must've thought: "what a dummy, I got her wrapped around my finger, great!'

And now as I sit and think things over, I should've never contemplated having you as a lover.

You put my life and health in jeopardy, and you constantly broke my heart and played mind games with me.

I wanted you to prove everyone wrong and I cried every time I heard a love song.

Not because I was in love with you, but because I didn't love me.

And that is some of the worst hurt that I could ever want for me.

And now that I have moved away, I hope that you will see it.

I had to stop communicating, because maybe if it is silent, you would finally hear it.

The tears I cried, were like a river

My heart being torn in half, I felt like it was being cut with a small, dull scissor.

There is no communication now, and I hope that it stays this way.

Because I allowed myself to go through this for years and I can't do it for one more day.

EROTIC

Before I started hosting, I did a lot of erotic poetry. This poem is only slightly erotic as opposed to what I normally used to recite. In any event, can you guess what I am talking about in my poem "I Gave You Passion?" It is not about another human at all.

Stay tuned…

I GAVE YOU PASSION

YOU GAVE ME PASSION,

It was an intense connection the moment I turned you on.

Our love was "low" at this point,

Like smooth jazz undertones playing behind a Common song.

YOU GAVE ME PASSION

It wasn't until you, that I knew how to make my own self feel good

And through every speed of the way, you provided comfort, just like you said that you would.

YOU GAVE ME PASSION

You accepted me although I had your brother first

I took the life out of him

Plugged you in and you know what's worse?

We move at a speed that me and your brother could never get to.

Causing me to tingle and pulsate and lift my head as if you were licking me too.

It's strange how you gave me this passion without me knowing your magnitude.

Or how I abruptly hang up the phone with my friends as rudely as I do.

I appreciate the fact that you allow my mind to wander and fantasize about the men who couldn't do what you do.

You gave me passion

It's funny how you know exactly what I want, but yet, I have never had a conversation with you.

YOU GAVE ME PASSION.

I GAVE YOU PASSION

I realized that you were a woman deprived of something precious for far too long.

I've been built to handle the pressure

I was built to last long.

I GAVE YOU PASSION

I love the thrill of his face being twisted because you allow him to watch.

Or how you choose to go a few rounds with me instead of punching a clock.

I GAVE YOU PASSION

Beat your box to me and I will make your hip hop slightly to the right.

I am the true definition of correctly allowing you to rock the mic.

I GAVE YOU PASSION

Your hill is like sugar, and I am a true female rappers delight.

I GAVE YOU PASSION

Handle with care or you just might chip your tooth tonight.

My bullet is silver, but I am a rabbit at best

And with my cousin made of jelly,

It's crazy to see how fast you undress

I GAVE YOU PASSION.

THE FIRST

Technically, the first poem I ever read in front of a crowd, was my poem entitled Weeping Willow. (My Dad helped me a little) I won first place at the library for it. So, from there, I just kept writing. I was nervous, but the following poem, "It All Came Out" was the first poem I ever did at an open mic. I even did a video for it on Market Street Mall, in Wilmington, Delaware, at a bar called 814. After I did this poem, some of the seasoned vets in the building told me that I did a really good job. The only critique was to put my paper down, memorize the poem and interact with the crowd. It took a minute, but I am there now…and then came Water.

IT ALL CAME OUT

See, it's been a while and I need to clear my head

I won't call out any names, Imma use scenarios instead.

I was hurt for a minute, but not because of why you may think

Hold up, let me back up-

IT ALL CAME OUT!

Okay, it started off smooth, I'm like: "this is the one"

Cause it didn't take much for you and I to have fun.

And maybe I was naive or too chill for you to handle

Cause you thought you broke me down,

But you did what every man do, or does, or whatever, check it

IT ALL CAME OUT

See it was on me because I gassed my own head

I was thinking "he will be back" then you came back and I was like "yeah that's what I thought!"

This is what I actually said.

But it was deeper than you boo

I was young and dumb and thought that what was in between my legs was gonna keep you

And it didn't, even though it's good

But check it, IT ALL CAME OUT

So, about the 10th time that I took you back, I started questioning myself like, does he really love me? Will he ever be true? Will he always come back?

You know, stuff like that.

Then I realized that I was talking to myself more than I talked to you

So, I became my own best friend.

I was tired of weeks passing and you not coming through and then when we would talk, I would say, "baby I miss you, can you come by? Maybe spend a little time?

And the response I got was "see this is just why" "you always naggin', you pushing me away"

And I was like "whoa, baby ok"

But check it-

IT ALL CAME OUT

So, then I found him and I treated him like you treated me

Ironic right?

And I kept the both of y'all

But with you, is where I wanted to be

But check it-

IT ALL CAME OUT

See, it started back when you said, "Yo, that shirt is hot."

I said, "This shirt right here, I had it for over a year."

And you said, "Well, I only see you when it's dark!"

I'm like damn

Is this the man I want to be with, the one I want to marry?

But I gave you a pass, hell I even laughed

Until you did the ultimate

But check it

IT ALL CAME OUT

See, if nothing else, I thought we had an understanding

I thought all of that gossiping stuff, wasn't a "man thing"

But when my business started coming back to me in the streets

I was like damn

Then my stomach started to hurt, and I thought, *"That's just my nerves."*

Until I went and got checked out and found out it was more than my nerves, it was something minor,

But in my heart, it was major.

And I was mad, but I had to smile

Because all the time I was heated with you, it came back to me that SHE really played you

And that's what you get and I ain't mad at all

Because I know that it's over, and I gave it my all

But check it

IT ALL CAME OUT!!

See this could've been worse and you put my life at risk

Cause it could have been so much more to what we had than this

But I cut them all off, I mean every last one.

The liar, the cheat, the possible "down low" one

And now I'm chillin' all by myself

And as for you, you got set up and you don't even see it.

And i should've known it was over because towards the end, the sex was so good and you was coming to my crib more than I wanted you too, messing up the flow of another coming through to see me.

And I never thought that I could feel this way, but you hear Omarion

"I got an Icebox"...

Yeah, you know the song

IT ALL CAME OUT

So now I'm free, free from you, free from him and free from her dirty twat

Who made your pockets hot

My mind is clear and I am on a whole other level

And I don't want to leave this Earth with my brain and feelings all disheveled

So, from me to all of you

Trust your gut from the start

Love yourself first

Be careful who you give your heart

Cuz this right here, can break you down

Some people do it like it's their craft, their art

But that's why

IT ALL CAME OUT

WATER

Water, that's my name, say it

Water

So smooth and so soothing, will you allow me to cleanse your soul?

Water, always refreshing even when I'm ice cold.

Water, taking all of the filth off of your body

Water

Everlasting, quenching your thirst when you taste this water.

Water

Realize while you are immersed within me, I am surrounding you with my water and now you are exposed within my water,

The same water you give to your sons and daughters

Water

More powerful than before because I have been enhanced by humans' water

Breaking down mountains

Water

Turning them into sand with no hands water

Why do you lust for me

Water

Trust me

Water

Drink me

Water

Need me

Water

Desire to feel me

Water?

Fill yourself up with my water, knowing you can't handle my water

Give in to my water

And my power is greater than you can ever imagine

Water

Causing excellent insulation with no Ions

Water

With any such impurity such as salt,

I can cause electricity readily as I can be split into constituent elements

Hydrogen and oxygen and allow a current to flow through me.

Water

And then when I freeze, causing the most unusual behavior- turning into a solid, hence my sister ice where I allow her to float on me

Water

Or maybe a gas, surrounding you with two times my molecular mass

Water

Putting out fires

Water

Hydrating,

Satisfying,

Soothing,

Essential,

Nourishing-

FEEL MY POWER

Water

SOMETIMES I JUST WRITE

SOMETIMES, I JUST WRITE...

He said get up off of your knees,

You don't have to do that, just yet

Let me sing to you first

Let me hold u

Get you...

Foreplay is different between us

Your lyrics with my rhythms

My strumming with your wordplay

Let me get on my knees and play this song I'm about to play

Let's talk about the mini you that I want to create when our foreplay is through

Let me caress and undress and hold u

Let's show love makers what love makers do

Let me rub you like a Djembe drum before our African ancestors lifted their hands to the sun

Like when a deal is finalized and the ink dries

Like when the stars, moon, and sun intertwine in the sky to become one.

Like before the dawn

Let me create a hew the color of moonlight that glows all over you through the clouds at night

Spreading love and light and love u right

So, I said Ok "You can be my valentine"

Although I don't believe In Cupid with his bow and arrows

I believe in love and reality

The hurt, the pain and frustration that comes with the aggravation of not being able to love u enough

The times when we think about giving up but decide to pray instead

As I rest my head on his chest and he says the magic words

"Let's get on our knees together, for our God has brought us together and we need to pray to permanently make this our forever."

Yes, Yes, Yes

This climax had nothing to do with the ultimate level of love because we rose above that.

Our lives have interlaced and overlapped to make us one.

Realizing we decided it's time to become...

And after all of his melodic notes

I said, "I do"

Jus Mee 2/14/2016

WORK CHRONICLES

You know how we run into these people at the job that we befriend because we are around them for most of the day? This poem is a little humorous and it touches on these work relationships that we build with people. It briefly address our interactions with our co-workers.

Enjoy…

CUBICLES

Our relationship started out very basic

"Pass the stapler please."

Then advanced to "What did you order? Can I taste it?"

We went from sharing pics to "Girl, let me tell you what he did!"

We went from talking about the kids and hating the job together so much that if one of us was absent, they would ask the other one "Do you know where she is?"

For 6 months, we were divided only by a cubicle

But for some reason, you were as close to me as my fam

That's why I find it strange that when our seats changed,

You no longer remembered my name.

Now it's apparent that the 8-10 hours out of the day that we spent together, didn't mean spit!

Someone else moved into your cubicle and they're already talking about how they are gonna quit.

For the life of me, I can't figure out how the whole job knows my biz.

First there was June, Sarah then Tara, Leroy, Mike, Jim, and Tony

And I was nice to them

But now they're all acting as if they don't know me.

Yet, everyone seems to be gossiping about me

And maybe I shouldn't have told them about me,

Even though they heard more about me from you.

The only thing that separated us was the cubicle I thought

But the truth is, a lesson was taught.

Just because I see you more than my family

We eat lunch together and you are always around me, doesn't make you my friend.

Even though we have a lot in common.

Our relationship started 6 months ago and we should have just remained cordial.

Because I allowed you to know my private side,

You took my business to a department on the other side.

Why would you tell the boss that Leroy slept with his wife?

How could Jane know that Sally was messing with Mike?

Now everyone is gossiping and looking at me, right?

But you was my cubicle friend.

And our relationship didn't have to change just because our seats were rearranged.

You sit near Tim now?

Oh, I see, he's your new best friend now?

Julie told me about your BBQ

She wanted to know why I didn't go.

She said the whole first floor was there

She was surprised I didn't know!

You want to start trouble?

I am going to tell her how you called her a Ho,

All because she was messing with Joe.

I'm telling him what you said about him too.

You're gonna wish you never sat in row 6, isle 2. Two seats back from the dude you said smells like piss.

You're gonna wish this cubicle divided us one more time, the way Imma run down the aisle and whip on your behind.

Wait till it's break time. HR is going to have to put us both out!

And don't go applying to the job I try and go to next.

I will tell them how your GED ain't real and that you are suing your boss from your last job, for trying to cop a feel.

You must not know this cubicle warfare stuff is real.

You can't be serious B

You moved away from me and now you can't stand me?

And to top it off, I introduced you to my family?

Don't try and beat me to the boss' office you B%^%!

THIS IS CUBICLE WAR

Stand up and face me you witch

Don't try and run out of the side door

Let's settle the score.

It's ten minutes left till the end of the day.

We acting like we are 5 years old with all of this "he say, she say"

Now here comes an email from you

I wonder what you gotta say

"Girl, I know you think that it's me, but I was mad about what Stacey told me you said about me. I know that I have been cold, but Troy told me what he was told. This is petty and you're my friend. Tomorrow my seat moves next to Justin and I have to admit with all this moving, my favorite seat was next to you and Susan. I think they moved me for talking to you too much. I don't want to fight no more so write me back Ok?

KIT-you know? Keep in touch!

Well, ain't this about some ish?

Troy said what? Stacey needs to quit. Girl I was mad, but I ain't trippin'.

They're moving my seat tomorrow too.

Guess who they put me next to?

YOU KNOW WHO!

Hurry up and shut down the computer.

Let's meet by the elevator

Let's approach Stacey and get things straight.

And the saga starts all over tomorrow at a quarter to 8.

THE CUBICLES…

A BIRTHDAY PARTY FOR JESUS

The concept of the following 2 poems came about because of my Aunt-Shirley Monroe. Aunt Shirley decided to throw a birthday party for Jesus. There were over 100 people in attendance. We had dinner, singing and it was a very informative day. On top of that, we did a toy drive and it was a success. I did the following 2 poems. I never shouted before in church. I did feel a fire inside of me this day, however. The words are simple, yet powerful.

These poems are dedicated to S. Monroe and K. Price (RIP)

BECAUSE HE ROSE

John 5:25-26 (KJV)

"Verily, verily, I say unto you, the hour is coming and now is, when the dead shall hear the voice of the Son Of God; and they that hear shall live. For as the Father hath life in himself, so hath he given to the son to have life in himself."

Death does not have to be the end!!

BECAUSE HE ROSE ON THE 3RD DAY-
He furnished the foundation of our faith.

BECAUSE HE ROSE ON THE 3RD DAY-
We have abundant life.

BECAUSE HE ROSE ON THE 3RD DAY-
We have agape love

BECAUSE HE ROSE ON THE 3RD DAY-
He restored our relationship with the Father.

BECAUSE HE ROSE ON THE 3RD DAY-

Everything was fulfilled that was written about him in the Laws of Moses.

BECAUSE HE ROSE ON THE 3RD DAY-
We recognize the power of God himself

BECAUSE HE ROSE ON THE 3RD DAY-
They couldn't say he wasn't who he really was.

BECAUSE HE ROSE ON THE 3RD DAY-
And according to Paul- "through him, everyone who believes is set free from every sin."

BECAUSE HE ROSE ON THE 3RD DAY-
We have salvation

BECAUSE HE ROSE ON THE 3RD DAY-
I know that my labor in the Lord is not in vain.

BECAUSE HE ROSE ON THE 3RD DAY-
And he's coming back again!!!

BECAUSE HE ROSE ON THE 3RD DAY!!

THE NATIVITY OF JESUS

Let me explain how this all began,

Adam caused some damage-

Jesus was born to fix it.

The traditional day of Jesus' birth is celebrated on 12/25

But I chose to celebrate him every day

Yes, I chose to celebrate him every day.

Somewhere between 6BC and 4BC,

Jesus was born to die for me!

How great is our God to impregnate Mary through the Holy Spirit at the verge of Joseph contemplating divorce?

All to save his people from their sins, he gave his life,

There is reason to REJOICE!!

Born in Bethlehem, symbolized by a shining star.

The Shepherds worshiped him as their Messiah and Lord- thanks to our Father God.

Paul, the Apostle, would refer to this birth as an event of cosmic significance which brought forth a "new man" who undid the damage caused by the first man-

But what does this birth mean to you?

Better yet, what should this birth mean to you?

Are you living righteous and Holy?
Are you living like God would want us too?
When you think about the birth of Jesus, do you remember not to judge?
Not to throw stones while you are in that glass house, do you remember to forgive, to be kind, to love?

Do you remember all that was sacrificed by one man and one man alone?

Glory to God- he was whipped and beaten; he was stoned!
Some mornings, I cry when I am blessed with a new day,
Another day to try and live right.
So, when we think about his birthday, some key words should come to mind,
Redemption, hope, salvation, love, promise and we need not take these things too light!

Happy birthday Jesus, we honor your day,
And I would like to personally thank you for sacrificing for me and my family.

CONCLUSION

I ended everything with two random poems I found, while looking through some papers. The first one is entitled "My Day." The story behind it is simple: once word got out in my family that I started doing open mics, and then hosting my own show, 302 LIVE, my Aunt called me. She asked me to come to her church and do two poems. Now, I had never done poems at church before, and normally, it was routine for me to have a few cocktails to settle my nerves before I went on stage. I mean, I am known to get on the stage and the first words out of my mouth are" "SHOUT OUT TO THE DRINKS!" But I am a firm believer that when family calls, you just go with no questions asked. I was scared this night in 2011. But my poem was received well.

I decided to end everything with my poem entitled "Be Happy." I believe that is what everyone should strive to do. If I could tell the younger me something that the older me has learned, it would be to not procrastinate when it comes to finding happiness. Don't let anyone steal happiness from you, and try and uplift those around you, so that they can feel happiness too. Don't change who you are, unless you are trying to be a better you. You won't be able to please everyone in life, so don't take it personal. Energy is everything. Work on your energy and build it up, so that the actions of others never breaks your spirit.

Be Blessed!!

MY DAY

When it's my time,

Rock my casket to a Louisiana old style, second line.

Play music that my family and friends can march and rejoice to.

Let the procession be a happy one.

Rain or shine, everyone will be glad to walk the streets as one.

Let the rhythm of the brass band play out loud.

"A closer walk with thee" to put my soul to rest.

Twirl a handkerchief in the air and strut your best.

Because I am going out with style.

God knows I tried my best.

Going to a place to reconnect with the best times in my life.

My family, my friends, and my God in that after life.

Let my blood continue to move through my kin here,

While my spirit lives on, way up there.

Cut my body loose down here.

No tears of sorrow, just happy tears for a better tomorrow.

Let the indigenous music of New Orleans play,

Like they've been doing at the Heritage festival since back in the day.

Because I am going to a place where I can eat Po' boys and crawfish beignets every day!

And the troubles of this cold, cold world will be so far away.

So, if I go, let it be that way.

Give me that Southern love,

and a down home Louisiana second line on

MY DAY

BE HAPPY

I need a booty like Erykah Badu.

I need you to see me from the front and realize what's about to pass you.

Then again, I need to be happy with what I got,

Like my hair.

And instead of wearing it like box braids

I need to be happy that its nappy with a mind of its own.

I need to be glad that I don't own a comb

I need to be happy that when he sees me in boy shorts, he smiles

I need to be happy that when I'm in my bra and panties, all tatted up in the mirror

I can still smile.

I need to be happy that I don't want to be at every club,

In every in crowd

Smokin' loud

Well maybe a pull or two

But I need to be happy that I can buy a bottle of wine

Set up 3 glasses and chill in my crib with a few

I need to be happy that I got to experience something other than today's norm

Like growing up with both of my parents in the same home

They're still together

I need to be happy that I got a job

It doesn't pay much, but-

I work hard

Well, most days I work hard but I got a job

And I need to be thankful that I'm not married yet

Because if he cheats on me

I'm gonna snap

As wet as my shit gets??!?

Like really dude?

I need to be happy I've had the same friends for over a decade

And I need to be happy with the newer friends I made

Because when things got rough,

Those new friends

Stepped up like old friends

And they showed me love and guided me the right way.

I need to be happy that I'm saying this to you

Because I can count on both hands

Some friends that didn't make it, can you?

And I need to be happy that God gave me a gift.

So, give thanks every day because there ain't no time like the present

BE HAPPY BE HAPPY BE HAPPY.

ABOUT THE AUTHOR

Jus Mee is a native New Yorker who has spent time in North Carolina, Virginia and Delaware, as well. She is the host of 302 Live The Ultimate Open Mic. She is passionate about her family, her friends and of course, her love for spoken word.

www.ingramcontent.com/pod-product-compliance
Lightning Source LLC
Chambersburg PA
CBHW021432070526
44577CB00001B/168